Africa

Africa presents an overview of the geography of this continent and its island countries. The teaching and learning in this unit are based on the five themes of geography developed by the Association of American Geographers together with the National Council for Geographic Education.

The five themes of geography are described on pages 2 and 3. The themes are also identified on all student worksheets throughout the unit.

Africa is divided into seven sections.

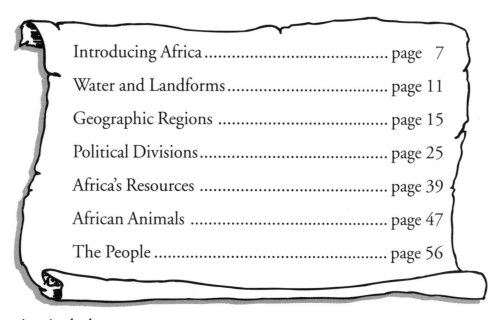

Each section includes:
* teacher resource pages explaining the activities in the section
* information pages for teachers and students
* reproducible resources
    maps
    note takers
    activity pages

Pages 4–6 provide suggestions on how to use this unit, including instructions for creating a geography center.

Congratulations on your purchase of some of the finest teaching materials in the world.

For information about other Evan-Moor products, call 1-800-777-4362 or FAX 1-800-777-4332

http://www.evan-moor.com

Author:	Jo Ellen Moore
Editor:	Jill Norris
Copy Editor	Cathy Harber
Desktop:	Keli Winters
Illustrator:	Cindy Davis
	Keli Winters
Cover Design:	Cheryl Puckett
Photography:	David Bridge, Digital Stock

Entire contents copyright ©1999 by EVAN-MOOR CORP.
18 Lower Ragsdale Drive, Monterey, CA 93940-5746
Permission is hereby granted to the individual purchaser to reproduce student materials in this book for noncommercial individual or classroom use only. Permission is not granted for school-wide, or system-wide, reproduction of materials.
Printed in U.S.A.

Evan-Moor
EDUCATIONAL PUBLISHERS

EMC 769

The Five Themes of Geography

·Location

Position on the Earth's Surface

Location can be described in two ways. **Relative location** refers to the location of a place in relation to another place. **Absolute location** (exact location) is usually expressed in degrees of longitude and latitude.

> We can say Gambia is located in the western part of Africa. Its boundaries are Senegal and the Atlantic Ocean.

> Bujumbura, the capital city of Burundi, is located at 3°S latitude, 29°E longitude.

·Place

Physical and Human Characteristics

Place is expressed in the characteristics that distinguish a location. It can be described in **physical characteristics** such as water and landforms, climate, etc., or in **human characteristics** such as languages spoken, religion, government, etc.

> South of the harsh northern deserts is the savanna, with short grasses and scattered trees.

> There are more than 1000 languages spoken in Africa.

·Relationships within Places

Humans and the Environment

This theme includes studies of how people depend on the environment, how people adapt to and change the environment, and the impact of technology on the environment. Cities, roads, planted fields, and terraced hillsides are all examples of man's mark on a place. A place's mark on man is reflected in the kind of homes built, the clothing worn, the work done, and the foods eaten.

> The majority of farmers in Africa live on small subsistence farms where families raise food and livestock for their own use.

 Movement

Human Interactions on the Earth

Movement describes and analyzes the changing patterns caused by human interactions on the Earth's surface. Everything moves. People migrate, goods are transported, and ideas are exchanged. Modern technology connects people worldwide through advanced forms of communication.

Egypt uses a network of pipelines to transport oil products and crude oil. These pipelines supply oil to refineries and export shipyards.

Regions

How They Form and Change

Regions are a way to describe and compare places. A region is defined by its common characteristics and/or features. It might be a geographic region, an economic region, or a cultural region.

Geographic region: The Sahara Desert stretches across the African continent from the Atlantic Ocean to the Red Sea.

Economic region: Copper is mined in a part of Africa that stretches across Zambia and into the Democratic Republic of the Congo (Zaïre).

Cultural region: The Tuareg are a matriarchal people living in the Sahara.

Using This Geography Unit

Good Teaching with *Africa*

Use your everyday good teaching practices as you present material in this unit.

- Provide necessary background and assess student readiness:
    - review necessary skills such as using latitude, longitude, and map scales
    - model new activities
    - preview available resources
- Define the task on the worksheet or the research project:
    - explain expectations for the completed task
    - discuss evaluation of the project
- Guide student research:
    - provide adequate time for work
    - provide appropriate resources
- Share completed projects and new learnings:
    - correct misconceptions and misinformation
    - discuss and analyze information

Doing Student Worksheets

Before assigning student worksheets, decide how to manage the resources that you have available. Consider the following scenarios for doing a page that requires almanac or atlas research:

- You have one classroom almanac or atlas.
  Make an overhead transparency of the page needed and work as a class to complete the activity, or reproduce the appropriate almanac page for individual students. (Be sure to check copyright notations before reproducing pages.)
- You have several almanacs or atlases.
  Students work in small groups with one resource per group, or rotate students through a center to complete the work.
- You have a class set of almanacs or atlases.
  Students work independently with their own resources.

Checking Student Work

A partial answer key is provided on pages 77 and 78. Consider the following options for checking the pages:

- Collect the pages and check them yourself. Then have students make corrections.
- Have students work in pairs to check and correct information.
- Discuss and correct the pages as a class.

         Africa • EMC 769

Creating a Geography Center

Students will use the center to locate information and to display their work.

Preparation

1. Post the unit map of Africa on an accessible bulletin board.
2. Add a chart for listing facts about Africa as they are learned.
3. Allow space for students to display newspaper and magazine articles on the continent, as well as samples of their completed projects.
4. Provide the following research resources:
   * world map
   * globe
   * atlas (one or more)
   * current almanac
   * computer programs and other electronic resources
   * fiction and nonfiction books (See bibliography on pages 79 and 80.)
5. Provide copies of the search cards (pages 69–71), crossword puzzle (pages 72 and 73), and word search (page 74). Place these items in the center, along with paper and pencils.

Additional Resources

At appropriate times during the unit, you will want to provide student access to these additional research resources:

* Filmstrips, videos, and laser discs
* Bookmarked sites on the World Wide Web (For suggestions, go to http://www.evan-moor.com and click on the Product Updates link on the home page.)

Making a Portfolio on Africa

Provide a folder in which students save the work completed in this unit.
Reproduce the following portfolio pages for each student:

- A Summary of Facts about Africa, page 66
  Students will use this fact sheet to summarize basic information they have learned about Africa. They will add to the sheet as they move through the unit.

- What's Inside This Portfolio?, page 67
  Students will record pages and projects that they add to the portfolio, the date of each addition, and why it was included.

- My Bibliography, page 68
  Students will record the books and other materials they use throughout their study of Africa.

At the end of the unit have students create a cover illustration showing some aspect of Africa.

Encourage students to refer to their portfolios often. Meet with them individually to discuss their learning. Use the completed portfolio as an assessment tool.

Using the Unit Map

Remove the full-color unit map from the center of this book and use it to help students do the following:

- locate and learn the names of landforms, water forms, and physical regions of Africa
- practice finding relative locations using the cardinal directions shown on the compass rose
- calculate distances between places using the scale

Introducing Africa

Tour the Geography Center

Introduce the Geography Center to your class. Show the research materials and explain their uses. Ask students to locate the sections of atlases and almanacs containing material about Africa.

Tanzanian

Thinking about Africa

Prepare a KWL chart in advance. Reproduce page 8 for each student. Give students a period of time (5–10 minutes) to list facts they already know about Africa and questions about the continent they would like answered.

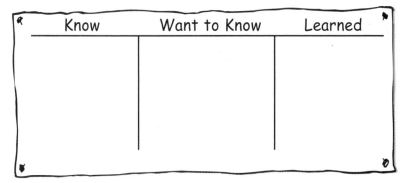

Know	Want to Know	Learned

Transfer their responses to the KWL chart. Post the chart in a place where you can add to it throughout your study of the continent.

Where Is Africa?

Reproduce pages 9 and 10 for each student.

"Locating Africa" helps students locate Africa using relative location. Use the introductory paragraph to review the definition of relative location, and then have students complete the page.

"Name the Hemisphere" reviews the Earth's division into hemispheres. Students are asked to name the hemispheres in which Africa is located. Using a globe to demonstrate the divisions, read the introduction together. Then have students complete the page.

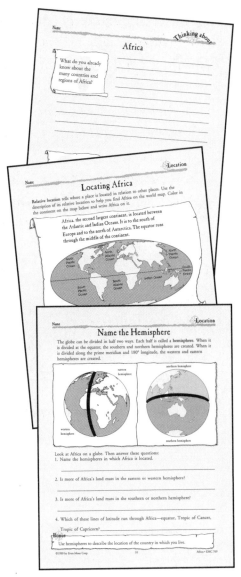

Africa

What do you already know about the many countries and regions of Africa?

_____
_____
_____
_____

_____
_____
_____
_____

If you could talk to someone from an African country, what would you ask?

_____
_____
_____
_____
_____

_____
_____
_____
_____

Name _____

Locating Africa

Relative location tells where a place is located in relation to other places. Use the description of its relative location to help you find Africa on the world map. Color in the continent on the map below and write Africa on it.

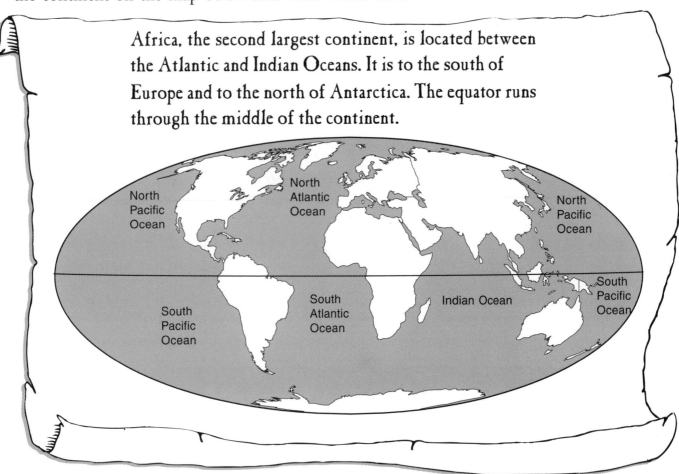

Africa, the second largest continent, is located between the Atlantic and Indian Oceans. It is to the south of Europe and to the north of Antarctica. The equator runs through the middle of the continent.

North Pacific Ocean

North Atlantic Ocean

North Pacific Ocean

South Pacific Ocean

South Atlantic Ocean

Indian Ocean

South Pacific Ocean

Look at a map of Africa. Find these places and write their relative locations:

1. Chad _____

_____

2. Lake Victoria _____

_____

Bonus

Imagine you are describing the relative location of the country in which you live to a student in Africa. What would you say?

Name the Hemisphere

The globe can be divided in half two ways. Each half is called a **hemisphere**. When it is divided at the equator, the southern and northern hemispheres are created. When it is divided along the prime meridian and 180° longitude, the western and eastern hemispheres are created.

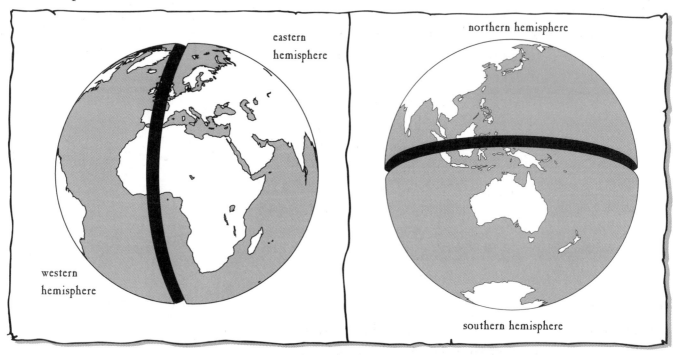

Look at Africa on a globe. Then answer these questions:

1. Name the hemispheres in which Africa is located.

_____

2. Is more of Africa's land mass in the eastern or western hemisphere?

_____

3. Is more of Africa's land mass in the southern or northern hemisphere?

_____

4. Which of these lines of latitude run through Africa—equator, Tropic of Cancer,

Tropic of Capricorn? _____

Bonus

Use hemispheres to describe the location of the country in which you live.

Water and Landforms

Collecting information by reading physical maps involves many skills. Pages 12–14 provide students with the opportunity to refine these skills as they learn about water and landforms on the continent of Africa.

Water Forms

Reproduce pages 12 and 13 for each student. Use the unit map to practice locating oceans, seas, lakes, and rivers on a map.

- Review how rivers and lakes are shown on a map.
- Discuss pitfalls students may face in finding the correct names (names written along the river, small type, several names close together).
- Have students locate at least one example of each type of water form on the unit map.
- Then have students locate and label the listed water forms on their individual physical maps.

Landforms

Reproduce page 14 for each student. Have students use the same map used to complete page 13, or reproduce new copies of page 12 for this activity.

- Review the ways mountains, deserts, and other landforms are shown on a map (symbols, color variations, labels).
- Have students practice locating some of the mountains, deserts, and other landforms on the unit map of Africa.
- Then have students locate and label the listed landforms on their individual physical maps.

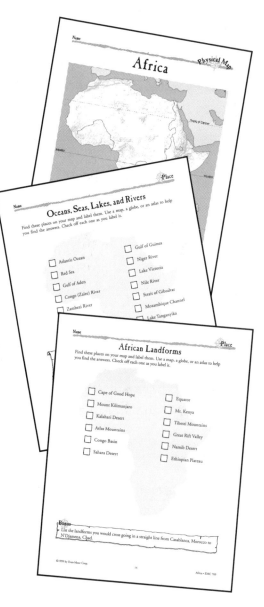

Name

Africa

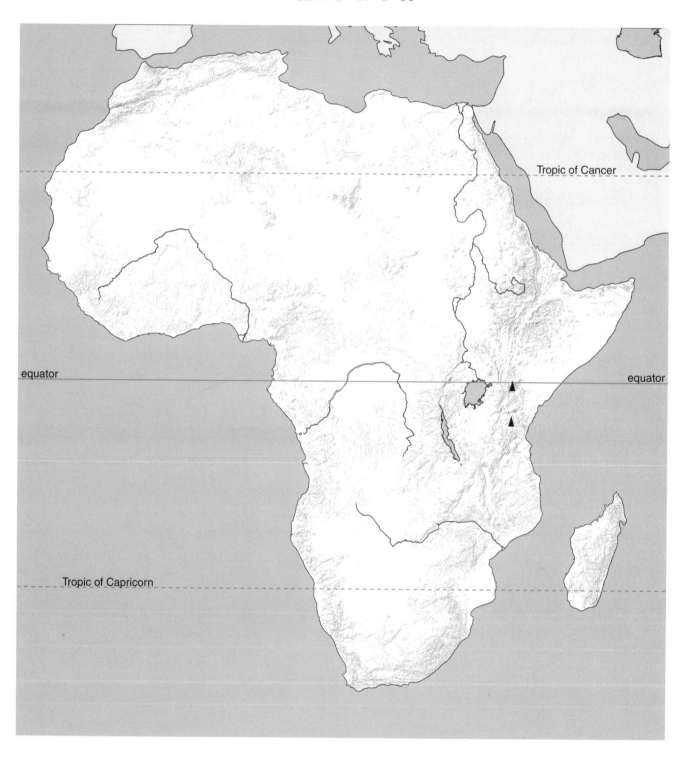

Tropic of Cancer

equator

equator

Tropic of Capricorn

12

Oceans, Seas, Lakes, and Rivers

Find these places on your map of Africa and label them. Use a map, a globe, or an atlas to help you find the answers. Check off each one as you label it.

☐ Atlantic Ocean   ☐ Gulf of Guinea

☐ Red Sea   ☐ Niger River

☐ Gulf of Aden   ☐ Lake Victoria

☐ Congo (Zaïre) River   ☐ Nile River

☐ Zambezi River   ☐ Strait of Gibraltar

☐ Indian Ocean   ☐ Mozambique Channel

☐ Mediterranean Sea   ☐ Lake Tanganyika

Trace the rivers dark blue.

Color the lakes dark blue.

Color the seas, oceans, and gulfs light blue.

Bonus

Imagine you are traveling by water from Cairo, Egypt, to Maputo, Mozambique. Explain the route you would follow.

African Landforms

Find these places on your map of Africa and label them. Use a map, a globe, or an atlas to help you find the answers. Check off each one as you label it.

☐ Cape of Good Hope

☐ Mount Kilimanjaro

☐ Kalahari Desert

☐ Atlas Mountains

☐ Congo Basin

☐ Sahara Desert

☐ Equator

☐ Mount Kenya

☐ Tibesti Mountains

☐ Great Rift Valley

☐ Namib Desert

☐ Ethiopian Highlands

Bonus

List the landforms you would cross going in a straight line from Casablanca, Morocco, to N'Djamena, Chad.

Geographic Regions

The continent of Africa has several geographic regions. Each has distinct physical characteristics and climatic conditions. The material on pages 16–24 explores some of these regions.

Regions of Africa

Follow the same procedure for each of these regions:

Sahara Desert, pages 16 and 17
Rainforests, pages 18 and 19
Savannas, pages 20 and 21

* Reproduce the required pages for each student.
* As a class, discuss the information about the region and find it on the map.
* Share additional information from books and videos in your geography center.
* Then have students answer the questions about the region on their activity pages.

Comparing Regions

Reproduce page 22 for each student. Students are to fill in the chart to compare and contrast characteristics of an African desert, a rainforest, and a savanna. They should recall the information they learned in the previous activity and do additional research using materials provided in the geography center.

Then have students select one of the regions on the chart, synthesize the information they have gathered, and write a report about the region.

Desertification

Reproduce pages 23 and 24 for each student. Make an overhead transparency of page 24. As a class, read and discuss the information, referring to the map to see where deserts currently exist and where there is danger of desertification. Send students to class resources to find out more about this problem and how countries are dealing (or not dealing) with it. Challenge students to think about ways to prevent desertification.

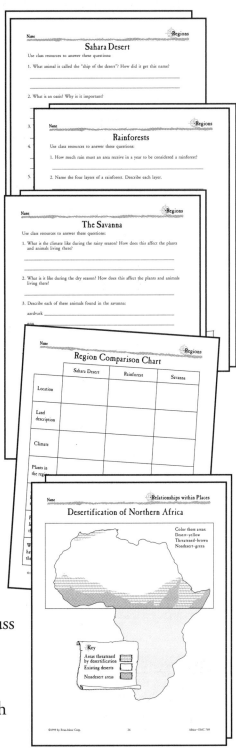

Sahara Desert

The Sahara Desert is one of the main geographical regions of Africa.

The Sahara desert is the largest desert in the world. It extends across northern Africa from the Atlantic Ocean to the Red Sea. It stretches more than 1200 miles (1931 km) from north to south. It is almost as large as the whole United States!

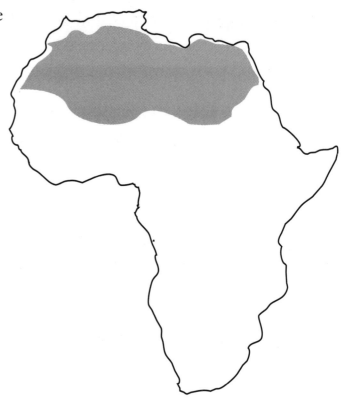

Barren rocky plateaus and gravelly plains make up most of the Sahara. The rest consists of vast areas of sand that lie within large basins. This is where some of the largest sand dunes in the world are found.

Even though the Sahara is very hot and dry, there are areas where water is found. These **oases** lie throughout the Sahara. The water in these areas comes from natural wells or springs. Towns have grown up around the largest oases.

Despite the lack of water, the Sahara has some scattered plant and animal life. The plants and animals have developed ways to live with limited water.

Some people who live in the Sahara raise crops irrigated by water from the oases. Others raise flocks of goats, sheep, and camels. They find grass for their stock along the desert's edges or in areas of recent rainfall. The herders have a nomadic life, living in tents that can be moved as soon as the grass has been eaten.

Today, modern transportation, such as cars and trucks, is used in some areas. Several roads, covered in a tar that can withstand the heat, cross the desert from north to south, and airports have been built at the largest oasis towns and at oil and gas fields.

Sahara Desert

Use class resources to answer these questions:

1. What animal is called the "ship of the desert"? How did it get this name?

_____

_____

2. What is an oasis? Why is it important?

_____

_____

3. What do desert nomads use for food?

_____

4. What adaptations allow plants to live in areas with so little rainfall?

_____

_____

5. Name one Saharan animal in each category:

mammal _____   amphibian_____

bird_____   reptile _____

6. Name a tree that grows in the Sahara Desert.

_____

Bonus

Describe some of the changes that have occurred in the Sahara since the discovery of petroleum.

Rainforests

There are large areas of rainforest in Africa. The largest rainforests are in the center and west of the continent, especially in Congo, Gabon, Cameroon, Nigeria, the Democratic Republic of the Congo, and Côte d'Ivoire. There are also rainforests on the island of Madagascar.

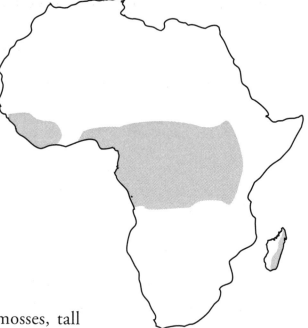

The rainforest climate is very hot and humid and is characterized by high amounts of rainfall. These conditions encourage abundant plant growth in the rainforests. Each layer of the rainforest has unique plants adapted to the amount of light and moisture the layer receives.

The rainforest is filled with shrubs, ferns and mosses, tall evergreens, palm trees, and numerous kinds of tropical hardwood trees. Many common houseplants originally came from Africa's rainforests. Many trees used for timber grow there. Some of the foods we eat were first discovered in the rainforest. Many medicines used today originated from rainforest plants.

The trees in the rainforest provide a habitat for many animals. Land-dwelling animals such as the okapi move among the trees eating fruit, leaves, ferns, and other types of plant foods. Civets and monkeys live and forage in the trees. Moles and rodents dig among the roots. Thousands of birds, spiders, insects, and snakes live in, on, and under the trees.

People have lived in the rainforests for thousands of years. Contact with the people from other, more developed areas has brought change to the ethnic groups still found in the rainforests. One group that continues to live as it always has is the Mbuti. Their small camps are found along the equator in the Democratic Republic of the Congo.

Rainforests

Use class resources to answer these questions:

1. How much rain must an area receive in a year to be considered a rainforest?

_____

2. Name the four layers of a rainforest. Describe each layer.

_____

_____

_____

_____

3. The African rainforest grows in the Congo Basin. What large river and its tributaries run through the basin?

_____

4. Name one African rainforest animal in each category:

   mammal _____   amphibian _____

   bird _____   reptile _____

5. Name a tree that grows in the African rainforest. _____

6. What is the main reason rainforests are being cut down?

_____

_____

Bonus

Describe one forest found in the country in which you live.

Savannas

The savannas of East Africa are flat, sunny plains covered in grass and scattered bushes and trees.

The savannas are home to many of the large mammals of Africa. Vast herds of zebras, gazelles, wildebeests, and various kinds of antelope come to graze on the grass. Elephants and giraffes eat the leaves and twigs off the trees.

Predators such as lions and cheetahs live on the savannas too. Scavengers such as vultures wait for the predators' leftovers.

Today, in many parts of the savannas, these wild animals are found only in game reserves, as cattle and sheep ranches have spread across the grasslands.

Wildebeests

Savannas

Use class resources to answer these questions:

1. What is the climate like during the rainy season? How does this affect the plants and animals living there?

_____

_____

2. What is it like during the dry season? How does this affect the plants and animals living there?

_____

3. Describe each of these animals found in the savannas:

   aardvark _____

   gnu _____

   kudu _____

   gazelle _____

4. Name one African animal found in the savannas from each of these categories:

   mammal _____   amphibian _____

   bird _____   reptile _____

5. What is the name of the thorn tree that grows in the savannas?

   _____

Bonus

The savannas are one type of grassland. Describe a type of grassland found in the country in which you live.

Region Comparison Chart

	Sahara Desert	Rainforest	Savanna
Location			
Land description			
Climate			
Plants in the region			
Animals living in the region			
People living in the region			
Ways people have changed the region			

Desertification

Before

After

Along the edges of deserts, fertile lands can become deserts. This is called **desertification.** Desertification can happen in several ways.

People can damage the land by misuse. They cut down too many trees, exposing land surface to wind and rain. They allow herds of animals to overgraze the land. They plant the same fields so often that the soil is worn out.

Wind and rain can damage the land. Erosion occurs when the fertile topsoil is blown or washed away. Very little can grow once the topsoil is gone.

The damage starts small but can spread into acres where nothing can grow. Millions of acres of land around the world are becoming deserts every year.

Bonus

Learn about deserts in the country in which you live. Has desertification become a problem?

Desertification of Northern Africa

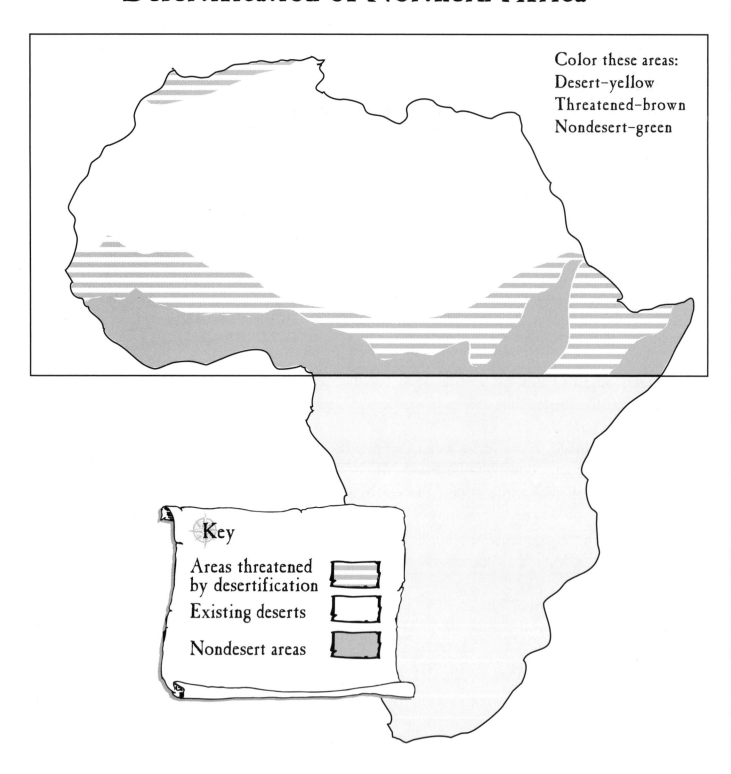

Color these areas:
Desert–yellow
Threatened–brown
Nondesert–green

Key

Areas threatened by desertification

Existing deserts

Nondesert areas

Political Divisions

A political map shows boundaries between countries, states, or territories. In this section students will use political maps to learn the countries of Africa and their capital cities, to calculate distance and direction, and to locate places using longitude and latitude.

The Countries of Africa

Reproduce pages 27 and 28 for each student. Have students use map resources to list the countries and then label them on the map.

Many African countries are small, with some island countries being mere dots on the map. Have students explore ways they might label these countries (draw a line from the country to open space, number or color-code the small countries and make a key at the bottom of the map, write the names of island countries in the water next to them, etc.).

Note: You will find "Western Sahara" on maps of Africa. Its ownership is being disputed by Morocco and a separatist movement. At the present time it is being administered by Morocco.

Country Names

Name the Countries

Reproduce page 29 for each student. Review the term "relative location." Have students use maps and atlases to name the countries described. They are then to write the relative location of several African countries.

Name Changes

Reproduce page 30 for each student. Read and discuss the introductory material on the page together. If you have access to both older and newer maps or atlases, show students examples of changes in borders and names. (The addition of Eritrea as an independent nation and the change in name from Zaïre to the Democratic Republic of the Congo are two examples occurring in the last few years.) Discuss possible reasons for these changes.

Note: This is a great time for students to use the World Wide Web to collect current information.

Part A of the activity page asks students to give the complete name of each country listed (Kenya–Republic of Kenya). Part B asks students to match the old name of several countries to the current name (French Cameroon–Cameroon).

Northern Africa

Capital Cities

Reproduce page 31 for each student. Have students use map resources to name the capital cities of the countries of Northern Africa and label them on the map.

Using a Compass Rose

Reproduce page 32 for each student. Use the compass rose on the unit map to review how to determine location using cardinal directions. Then have students complete the activity independently, using their maps of Northern Africa (page 31).

Western, Central, and Eastern Africa

Capital Cities

Reproduce page 33 for each student. Have students use map resources to name the capital cities of the countries of Western, Central, and Eastern Africa and label them on the map.

Longitude and Latitude

Reproduce page 34 for each student. Use a map to review how to use lines of longitude and latitude to determine exact locations. Then have students complete the activity independently, using their maps of Western, Central, and Eastern Africa (page 33).

Southern Africa

Capital Cities

Reproduce page 35 for each student. Have students use map resources to name the capital cities of the countries of Southern Africa and label them on the map.

How Far Is It?

Reproduce page 36 for each student. Use the unit map to review how to use a map scale to figure distances. Then have students use a ruler and the map scale to determine the distance between the listed places (page 35).

Country Fact Sheet

Make an overhead transparency of page 37. Reproduce page 38 for each student. Have students refer to the transparency as you ask questions that can be answered by the information on the fact sheet.

Have students help create a file of fact sheets for the countries in Africa. Have each student select a different country to research. Allow time for students to share what they discover about their countries. Keep the completed sheets in a binder in the geography center.

Africa

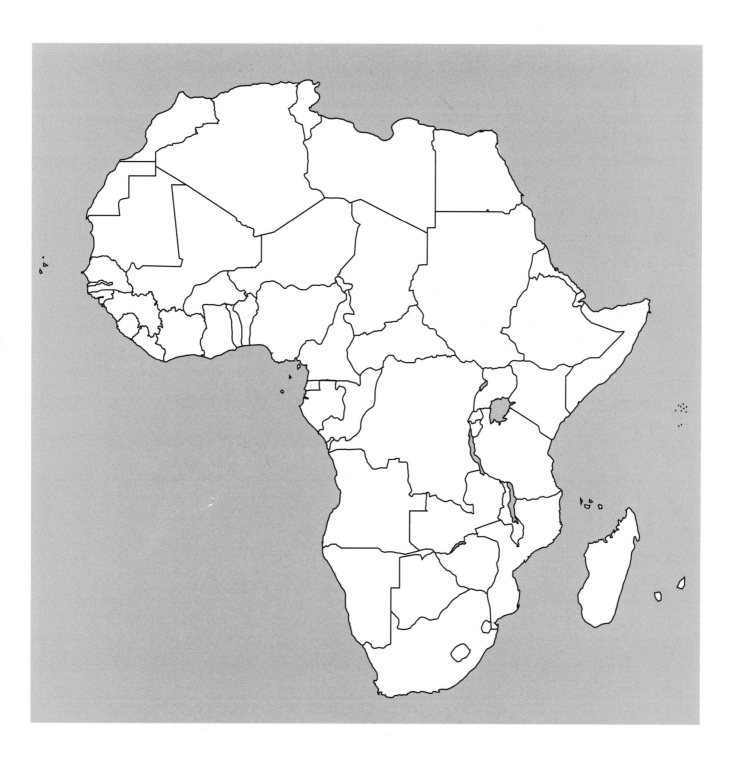

The Countries of Africa

List all the countries in Africa. Start the list with all the countries you can name. Use class map resources to help you complete the list. (Don't forget the island countries.) Then label the countries on the map.

_____   _____   _____

_____   _____   _____

_____   _____   _____

_____   _____   _____

_____   _____   _____

_____   _____   _____

_____   _____   _____

_____   _____   _____

_____   _____   _____

_____   _____   _____

_____   _____   _____

_____   _____   _____

_____   _____

Name the Countries

Read the relative location and name the country.

1. This country is located on the northeastern side of Africa. Sudan, Ethiopia, and the Red Sea border it.

   Name the country. _____

2. Kenya, Sudan, Tanzania, Rwanda, and the Democratic Republic of the Congo surround this small country. Lake Victoria forms one of its borders.

   Name the country. _____

3. This small, narrow country is in western Africa on the Gulf of Guinea. It is between Ghana and Benin.

   Name the country. _____

4. This country in northwestern Africa is the home of ancient pyramids. It touches both the Mediterranean Sea and the Red Sea.

   Name the country. _____

5. This small country in southern Africa is completely surrounded by South Africa.

   Name the country. _____

6. Mt. Kilimanjaro, the highest point in Africa, is in this country located on the eastern coast of Africa.

   Name the country. _____

Write the relative locations of these African countries:

1. Chad _____

2. Algeria _____

3. Mali _____

4. Madagascar _____

Name Changes

When looking at several maps or atlases, you may notice different names on the same country. This can happen for several reasons:

• It may be called one name in the language you speak and another name in the native language of the country.

• It may have a formal name that is longer than the common name more often used.

• The name of the country may have changed since the map you are using was produced.

A. Use an atlas, a world almanac, and the World Wide Web to find the complete name for the following countries:

1. Tanzania _____   5. Eritrea _____

2. Comoros _____   6. Gabon _____

3. Congo _____   7. Libya _____

4. Egypt _____   8. Mauritania _____

B. Match to show which countries were once called by these names:

1. Dahomey   Zimbabwe
2. Southern Rhodesia   Ghana
3. Zaïre   Côte d'Ivoire
4. Ivory Coast   Burkina Faso
5. Gold Coast   Benin
6. Upper Volta   Democratic Republic of the Congo

Bonus

Has your country ever had a different name? Try to find out.

Name

Northern Africa

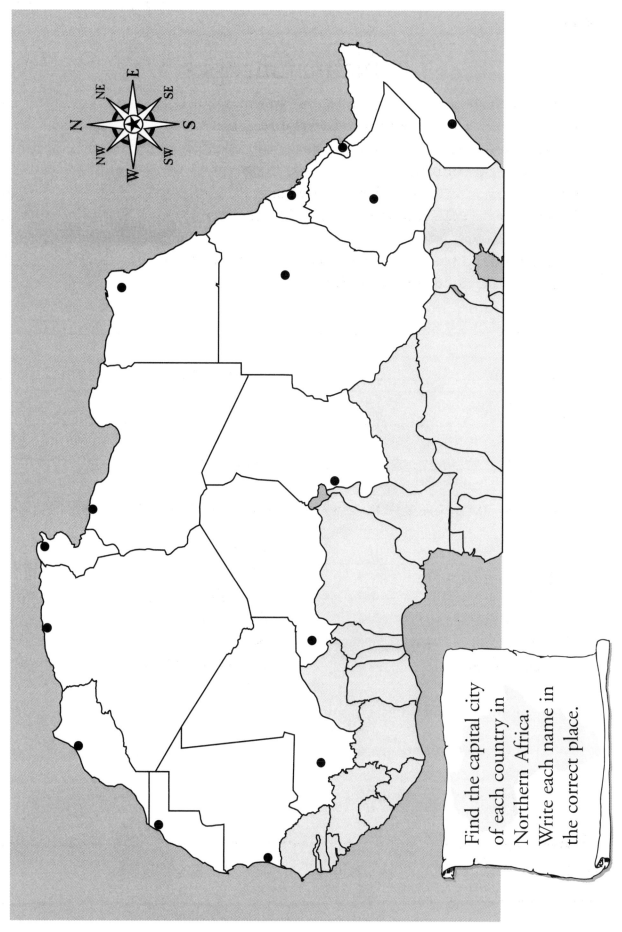

Find the capital city of each country in Northern Africa. Write each name in the correct place.

Using a Compass Rose

Many maps include a **compass rose**.
A compass rose shows the cardinal
directions—north, south, east, and
west. It can be used to describe
relative locations.

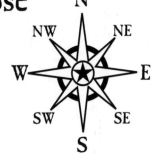

A. Use the compass rose on your map to find the direction you would travel between
the cities listed below.

From	To	Direction
Tunis, Tunisia	Tripoli, Libya	
Cairo, Egypt	Bamako, Mali	
Niamey, Niger	Djibouti, Djibout	
Addis Ababa, Ethiopia	Khartoum, Sudan	
N'Djamena, Chad	Rabat, Morocco	
Nouakchott, Mauritania	Asmara, Eritrea	
Algiers, Algeria	Khartoum, Sudan	
Asmara, Eritrea	Bamako, Mali	

B. Use the compass rose to answer these questions:

1. If you travel north from Chad, what sea will you reach? _____

2. If you travel east from Djibouti, what gulf will you reach? _____

3. If you travel west from Niger, what ocean will you reach? _____

4. If you travel east from Egypt, what sea will you reach? _____

Bonus
Imagine you are flying in a straight line from your hometown to Egypt. In which
direction would you travel?

Western, Central, and Eastern Africa

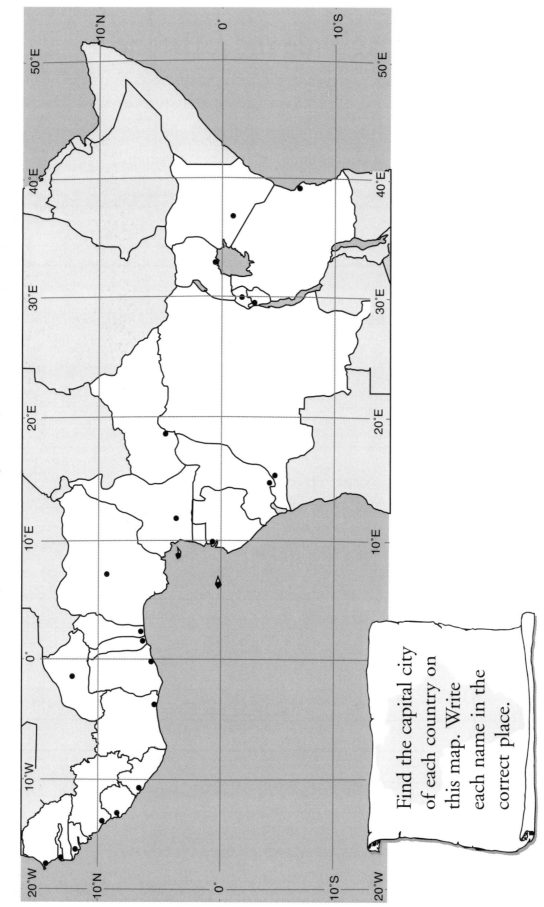

Find the capital city of each country on this map. Write each name in the correct place.

Longitude and Latitude

Lines of longitude and latitude are used to find exact (absolute) locations of places on the continent. Use the lines of longitude and latitude on your map to answer these questions:

A.

1. Which capital cities are located west of 0° (prime meridian)?

_____

_____

_____

2. Which capital cities are located east of 0° (prime meridian)?

_____

_____

_____

3. Which island country is located closest to 0°,0°?

_____

B. Find what capital city is located at these points.

Latitude	Longitude	Location
7°S	39°E	
1°S	37°E	
15°N	17°W	
2°S	30°E	
6°N	0°	
0°	33°E	

Bonus

Write the exact (absolute) location of your hometown using longitude and latitude.

Southern Africa

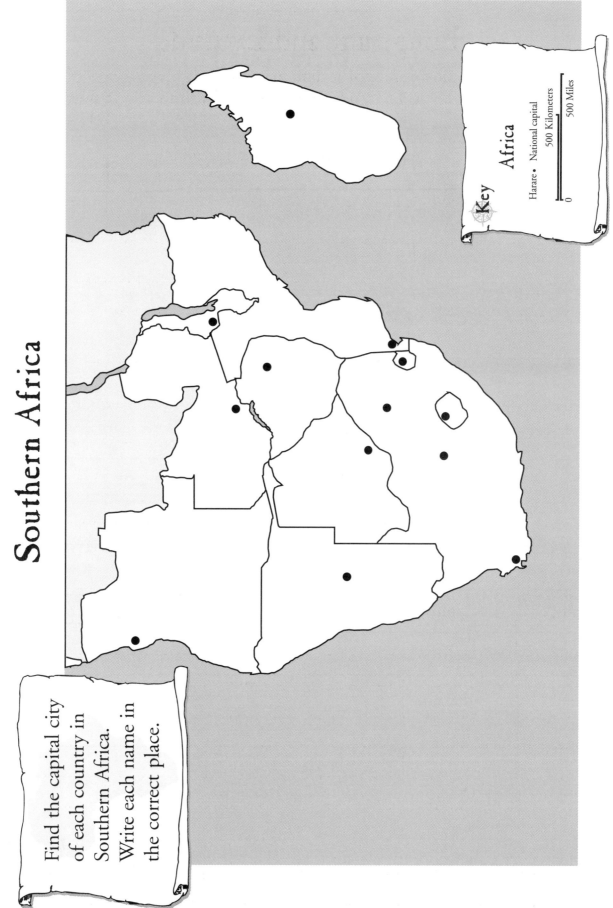

Key

Africa

Harare • National capital

500 Kilometers

500 Miles

0

Find the capital city of each country in Southern Africa. Write each name in the correct place.

How Far Is It?

A **linear** or **distance scale** is used to measure the distance between two places on a map.

Use a ruler and the map scale to help you measure the distance between these locations.

From	To	Distance
Luanda	Swaziland	
Lusaka	Windhoek	
Maseru	Gaborone	
Lilongwe	Luanda	
Antananarivo	Harare	
Maputo	Mbabane	
Gaborone	Pretoria	

Now find two places on the map that are about 100 miles (161 km) apart.

Bonus

Imagine you are planning to visit Dakar, Senegal. Use the distance scale on a world map to calculate how far it is from your hometown to Dakar.

Name of country	
United Republic of Tanzania	Country Fact Sheet

Capital city __Dar es Salaam__

Land area __364,017 square miles__

Population __29,460,753__

Major languages spoken

__Kiswahili or Swahili, English,__
__Arabic, many local languages__

Natural resources, crops, industries

__sisal, cotton, coffee, tobacco,__
__diamond and gold mining, oil__
__refining, cement, textiles,__
__fertilizer/insecticide (made__
__from chrysanthemums)__

Physical description of the country

__plains along the eastern coast; central__
__plateau; highlands in the north and__
__south; the Serengeti, Ngorongoro__
__Crater, and Lake Victoria__

Interesting plants and animals

__grasslands with grasses, bushes, and__
__acacia trees; forests with ferns,__
__mosses, and many kinds of trees; lions,__
__elephants, black rhinos, monkeys__

Facts about the people living there

__99% Black Africans, mostly__
__Bantu; 1% other peoples—__
__Arabian, Asian, and European__

Draw the country's flag here.

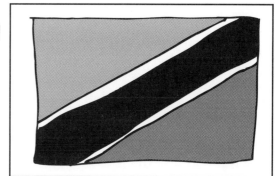

Name of country

Country Fact Sheet

Capital city_____

Land area_____

Population _____

Major languages spoken

_____

_____

_____

Natural resources, crops, industries

_____

_____

_____

Physical description of the country

_____

_____

_____

_____

Interesting plants and animals

_____

_____

_____

_____

Facts about the people living there

_____

_____

_____

_____

_____

Draw the country's flag here.

Africa • EMC 769

Africa's Resources

This series of activities introduces students to the natural and man-made resources of Africa.

Resources

Prepare for this lesson by enlarging the political map on page 27, using an overhead projector and a sheet of butcher paper. Post the map on a bulletin board.

Reproduce page 41 for each student. Assign one or more countries to each student. Have them use atlases, almanacs, and books to locate information about the natural resources, crops and livestock, and manufactured goods of the country or countries they have been assigned. Students are to record the information gathered on their activity sheets.

Create a "key" on the map using symbols agreed upon by the students. Then have students place symbols for the items on their lists in the appropriate locations on the large map of Africa.

African Agriculture

Reproduce page 42 for each student. As a class, read and discuss the material provided. Ask students who have family members involved in agriculture to share what they know about the growing and selling of crops and livestock.

Have each student select five countries in Africa to research using class resources. They are to compile lists of the agricultural products raised in each of the five countries. Compile the resulting information into a class list of African agricultural products.

Mineral Resources

Reproduce page 43 for each student. Minerals are an abundant natural resource in Africa. Challenge students to come up with a list of items that can be considered mineral resources (petroleum and natural gas, coal, copper, zinc, gold, diamonds, etc.). Have students use class resources to find the information about minerals needed to complete their activity pages.

Complete the lesson by discussing reasons for the slow development of these resources in some African countries (inadequate transportation systems, not enough monetary resources to develop the industry, political upheaval).

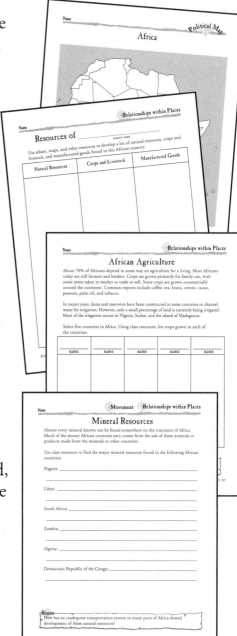

Agriculture, Service, and Industry

Reproduce pages 44 and 45 for each student. Make an overhead transparency of page 45. Explain that information about a place or a culture is often shown in graph form. Discuss the meanings of the terms agriculture (raising of crops and livestock), industry (manufacturing of goods), and service (fulfilling the public's needs) and what items fit into each category. Show the transparency and have students compare the percentages of each category for the six countries shown on the graph. Then have students complete the questions on the activity page.

Off to Africa

Come to Africa

Tourism is a big business in many parts of Africa. Visit a travel agency to get samples of brochures and posters about African trips. After sharing these materials, have students develop one of the following:

- a brochure of things to do on an African vacation
- a travel poster about one special place or site in Africa
- a list of ways to be a considerate tourist
- a video advertisement encouraging people to come to Africa

An African Vacation

Reproduce page 46 for each student. Students are to select a place to visit in Africa, explain their choice, and write a postcard they might send while on the imagined visit.

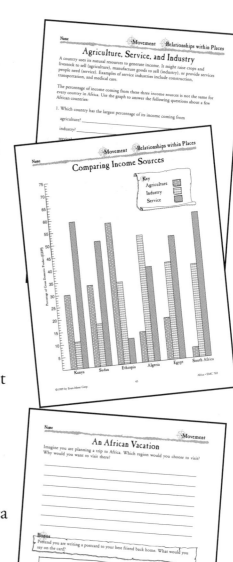

Resources of _____
country's name

Use atlases, maps, and other resources to develop a list of natural resources, crops and livestock, and manufactured goods found in this African country.

Natural Resources	Crops and Livestock	Manufactured Goods

African Agriculture

About 70% of Africans depend in some way on agriculture for a living. Most Africans today are still farmers and herders. Crops are grown primarily for family use, with some items taken to market to trade or sell. Some crops are grown commercially around the continent. Common exports include coffee, tea, fruits, cotton, cacao, peanuts, palm oil, and tobacco.

In recent years, dams and reservoirs have been constructed in some countries to channel water for irrigation. However, only a small percentage of land is currently being irrigated. Most of the irrigation occurs in Nigeria, Sudan, and the island of Madagascar.

Select five countries in Africa. Using class resources, list crops grown in each of the countries.

name	name	name	name	name

Bonus

What does a country need in order for more farmland to be irrigated?

Mineral Resources

Almost every mineral known can be found somewhere on the continent of Africa. Much of the money African countries earn comes from the sale of these minerals or products made from the minerals to other countries.

Use class resources to find the major mineral resources found in the following African countries:

Nigeria: _____

_____

Libya: _____

_____

South Africa: _____

_____

Zambia: _____

_____

Algeria: _____

_____

Democratic Republic of the Congo: _____

_____

Bonus
How has an inadequate transportation system in many parts of Africa slowed development of these natural resources?

Agriculture, Service, and Industry

A country uses its natural resources to generate income. It might raise crops and livestock to sell (agriculture), manufacture goods to sell (industry), or provide services people need (service). Examples of service industries include construction, transportation, and medical care.

The percentage of income coming from these three income sources is not the same for every country in Africa. Use the graph to answer the following questions about a few African countries:

1. Which country has the largest percentage of its income coming from

   agriculture? _____

   industry? _____

   service? _____

2. Which country has the least percentage of its income coming from

   agriculture? _____

   industry? _____

   service? _____

3. South Africa is considered a developed country. Ethiopia is a developing country. Compare the sources of income for these two countries. How are they alike? How are they different?

   _____

   _____

   _____

   _____

Bonus
   Name a manufactured product, an agricultural product, and a service provided in the state in which you live.

Comparing Income Sources

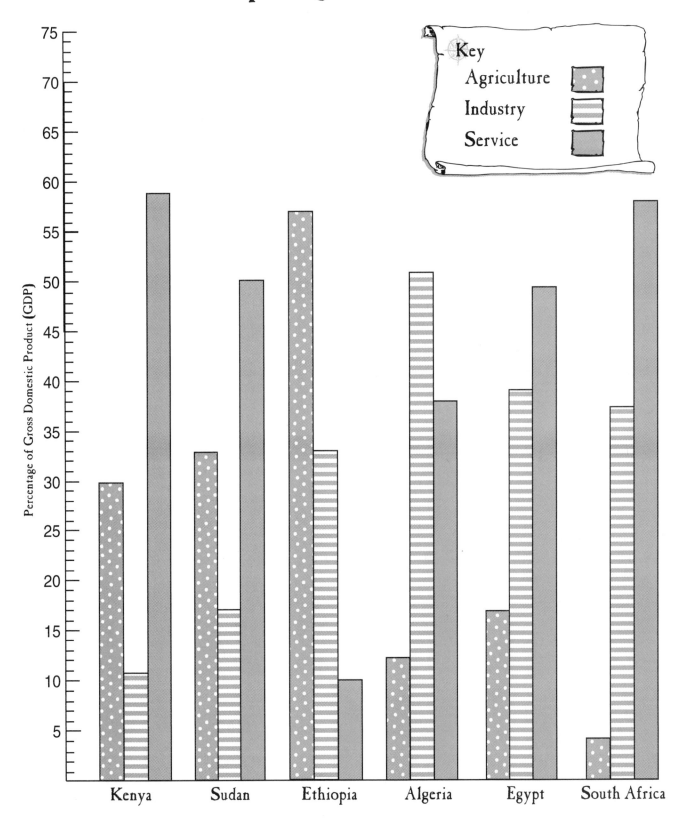

Key
Agriculture
Industry
Service

Percentage of Gross Domestic Product (GDP)

Kenya   Sudan   Ethiopia   Algeria   Egypt   South Africa

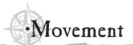

An African Vacation

Imagine you are planning a trip to Africa. Which region would you choose to visit? Why would you want to visit there?

_____

_____

_____

_____

_____

_____

_____

Bonus

Pretend you are writing a postcard to your best friend back home. What would you say on the card?

African Animals

Each region of Africa has its own unique animals. Some of the animals in Africa do not exist anywhere else on Earth. In this section students will learn about many of these animals.

Hyena

Introductory Activities

Begin by challenging students to name the African animals they know. List them on a chart and write a descriptive phrase after each name.

> elephant–the biggest land mammal, big ears and a long trunk
> lion–large wild cat, lives in a pride
> zebra–black and white stripes, looks kind of like a horse
> flamingo–pink bird with a long neck and long legs

Share books or show a video about African animals. Discuss information learned from these sources and add new animal names and descriptive phrases to the chart.

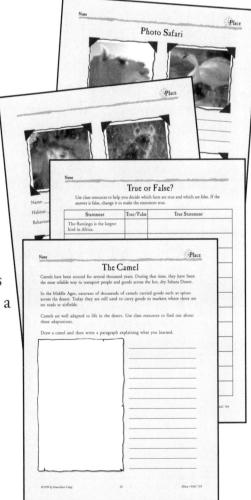

Wild Animals of Africa

Reproduce the following pages for each student:
- Photo Safari, pages 49 and 50

  "Photo Safari" asks students to imagine they have just returned from a photo safari in Africa and are putting their photographs in a scrapbook. Send students to class resources to find information about the animals in the "photos." Have them name the animals, identify each animal's habitat, and describe two of its behaviors.

- True or False?, page 51

  "True or False?" asks students to determine if statements about African animals are true or false, and then to give a reason for each selection.

- The Camel, page 52

  Students are to do research to discover and record what characteristics make it possible for a camel to live in the desert.

Endangered Animals

Animals in Danger

Reproduce page 53 for each student. As a class, brainstorm a list of African animals that students think are endangered. Record these on a chart. Then have students use class resources to find animals that are actually endangered. (These are to be listed on the student's activity page.) Compare student lists to the chart. Mark out any animals on the class chart that are not endangered.

Have each student create a poster informing people about one endangered animal.

Game Reserves

Reproduce page 54 for each student. Explain that many African countries are searching for ways to protect their endangered animals. One way this is being done is by the establishment of game reserves. The goal of these reserves is to provide a place where animals can live in safety. Have students use class resources to find out about some of these reserves and then complete the activity. Allow time for students to share what they learn with the class.

African Animal Report

Reproduce page 55 for each student. Students choose one interesting African animal and use class resources to locate information about the animal. They are to record what they learn on their note takers and then synthesize what they have learned into an oral or written report.

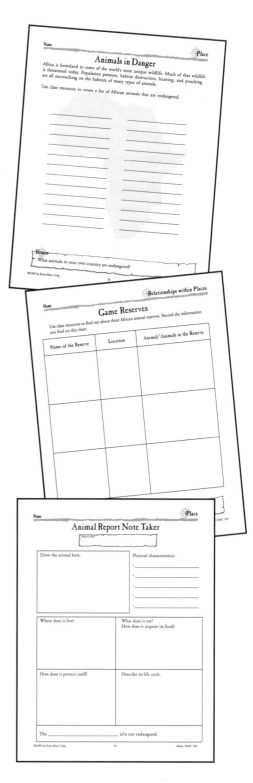

Photo Safari

Name: Dromedary

Habitat: _____

Facts:_____

_____

Name: Flamingo

Habitat: _____

Facts:_____

_____

Name: Gorilla

Habitat: _____

Facts:_____

_____

Name: Giraffe

Habitat: _____

Facts:_____

_____

Name: Okapi

Habitat: _____

Facts: _____

_____

Name: Hyena

Habitat: _____

Facts: _____

_____

Name: Chimpanzee

Habitat: _____

Facts: _____

_____

Name: Lion

Habitat: _____

Facts: _____

_____

True or False?

Use class resources to help you decide which facts are true and which are false. If the answer is false, change it to make the statement true.

Statement	True/False	True Statement
The flamingo is the largest bird in Africa.		
Chimpanzees are vegetarians.		
The lioness does most of the hunting for the pride.		
African elephants are larger than Asian elephants.		
A pangolin is a type of reptile.		
The cheetah is the fastest cat in Africa.		
Camels store water in their humps.		
An okapi grazes on grass.		
Adult gorillas live alone.		
The skin of a chameleon can change colors.		
A hippopotamus can stay underwater for a long time.		
An aardvark lives in a tree.		

The Camel

Camels have been around for several thousand years. During that time, they have been the most reliable way to transport people and goods across the hot, dry Sahara Desert.

In the Middle Ages, caravans of thousands of camels carried goods such as spices across the desert. Today they are still used to carry goods to markets where there are no roads or airfields.

Camels are well adapted to life in the desert. Use class resources to find out about these adaptations.

Draw a camel and then write a paragraph explaining what you learned.

Name

 ·Place

Animals in Danger

Africa is homeland to some of the world's most unique wildlife. Much of that wildlife is threatened today. Population pressure, habitat destruction, hunting, and poaching are all encroaching on the habitats of many types of animals.

Use class resources to create a list of African animals that are endangered.

_____   _____

_____   _____

_____   _____

_____   _____

_____   _____

_____   _____

_____   _____

_____   _____

_____   _____

Bonus

What animals in your own country are endangered?

Game Reserves

Use class resources to find out about three African animal reserves. Record the information you find on this chart.

Name of the Reserve	Location	Animal/Animals in the Reserve

Bonus

Find out about how endangered animals are being protected in your own country.

·Place

Animal Report Note Taker

Name of animal

_____

Draw the animal here.

Physical characteristics:

• _____

• _____

• _____

• _____

• _____

Where does it live?

What does it eat?
How does it get its food?

How does it protect itself?

Describe its life cycle.

The _____ is/is not endangered.

The People

Africa is considered the place where the first humans lived and learned to use tools. Today millions of people live there. It is a continent of many different ethnic groups and cultures. It is a continent where many changes are occurring. This section will introduce students to some of the people and some of the changes.

The People of Africa

Introduction

Invite speakers from Africa or of African descent to speak to the class. Prepare students for speakers by planning questions to ask. Appoint several students to record questions asked and answers received. Follow up the visit by writing thank-you letters.

Africa's Ethnic Groups

Reproduce page 58 for each student. As a class, read and discuss the information page. Students then use class resources to find out about several African ethnic groups.

Changes

Reproduce pages 59 and 60 for each student. As a class, read and discuss the information on page 59. Help students understand the concept of "less developed," "developing," and "developed" countries. Discuss what type of infrastructure is needed for these changes to occur (need a fairly stable economy, roads and train tracks, access to adequate electricity and water supplies, etc.). Students then complete the activity independently.

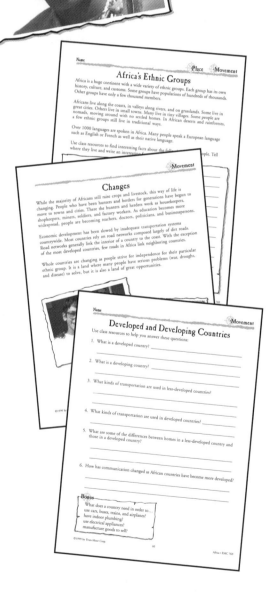

Information Graph

Reproduce page 61 for each student and also make an overhead transparency of the page. Show the transparency as you ask students questions about the population of people in various African countries. Challenge students to find reasons for the differences in the population sizes among the various countries.

People Report

Reproduce page 62 for each student. Challenge students to work in small groups, using a resource book to find the names of as many African ethnic groups as they can in a set period of time (15–30 minutes). Then list on the chalkboard the groups found. Have each student select one group to learn more about. Students use class and library resources to find information, record information on their note takers, and then synthesize the information into an oral or written report. Provide time for students to share what they've learned with the rest of the class.

African Music and Art Forms

Reproduce the following pages for each student:

• African Music, page 63

Check your school and public libraries for tapes or CDs of traditional African music. Share the music as you read and discuss the information on page 63. Have students study the pictures of instruments. Then ask them to explain how the instrument is played (plucked, shaken, beaten, blown).

• African Art Forms, page 64

Collect books of African art from the library. Share pictures of the various art forms (pottery, metal work, beads, baskets, fabrics). As a class, discuss the information on page 64. Extend the activity by providing clay and weaving materials for students to explore.

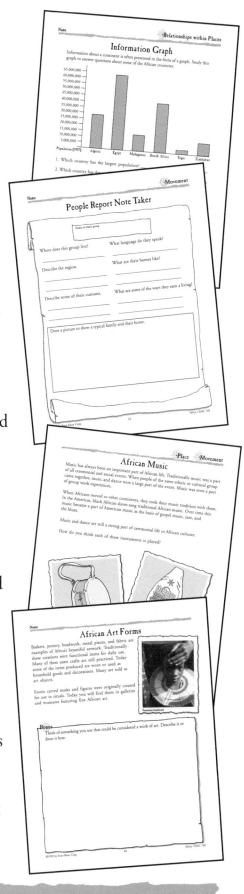

Name _____

Africa's Ethnic Groups

Africa is a huge continent with a wide variety of ethnic groups. Each group has its own history, culture, and customs. Some groups have populations of hundreds of thousands. Other groups have only a few thousand members.

Africans live along the coasts, in valleys along rivers, and on grasslands. Some live in great cities. Others live in small towns. Many live in tiny villages. Some people are nomads, moving around with no settled homes. In African deserts and rainforests, a few ethnic groups still live in traditional ways.

Over 1000 languages are spoken in Africa. Many people speak a European language such as English or French as well as their native language.

Use class resources to find interesting facts about the following African people. Tell where they live and write an interesting fact about them.

Maasai _____

_____

Egyptian _____

_____

Nigerian _____

_____

Mbuti _____

_____

San _____

_____

Taureg _____

_____

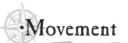

Changes

While the majority of Africans still raise crops and livestock, this way of life is changing. People who have been hunters and herders for generations have begun to move to towns and cities. There the hunters and herders work as housekeepers, shopkeepers, miners, soldiers, and factory workers. As education becomes more widespread, people are becoming teachers, doctors, politicians, and businesspersons.

Economic development has been slowed by inadequate transportation systems countrywide. Most countries rely on road networks composed largely of dirt roads. Road networks generally link the interior of a country to the coast. With the exception of the most developed countries, few roads in Africa link neighboring countries.

Whole countries are changing as people strive for independence for their particular ethnic group. It is a land where many people have serious problems (war, drought, and disease) to solve, but it is also a land of great opportunities.

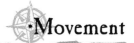

Developed and Developing Countries

Use class resources to help you answer these questions:

1. What is a developed country? _____

_____

2. What is a developing country? _____

_____

3. What kinds of transportation are used in less-developed countries?

_____

_____

4. What kinds of transportation are used in developed countries? _____

_____

5. What are some of the differences between homes in a less-developed country and those in a developed country?

_____

_____

6. How has communication changed as African countries have become more developed?

_____

_____

Bonus

What does a country need in order to...
* use cars, buses, trains, and airplanes?
* have indoor plumbing?
* use electrical appliances?
* manufacture goods to sell?

Information Graph

Information about a continent is often presented in the form of a graph. Study this graph to answer questions about some of the African countries.

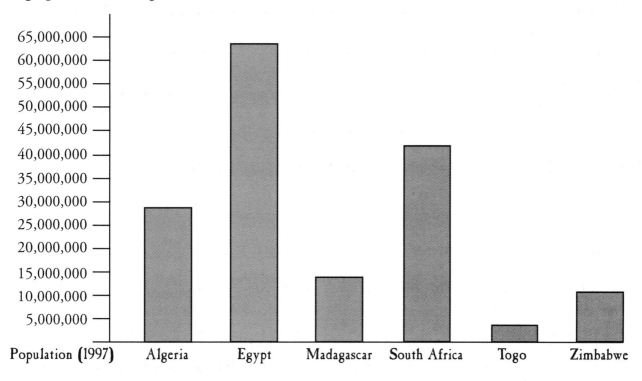

Population (1997)   Algeria   Egypt   Madagascar   South Africa   Togo   Zimbabwe

1. Which country has the largest population? _____

2. Which country has the smallest population? _____

3. What is the population difference between Egypt and Zimbabwe? _____

4. What is the population difference between Togo and South Africa? _____

Bonus

Use an almanac to:
- find the African country with the largest population
- find the African country with the smallest population

Add these figures to the graph.

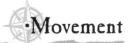
People Report Note Taker

Name of ethnic group

Where does this group live?

_____

Describe the region.

_____

_____

Describe some of their customs.

_____

_____

What language do they speak?

_____

What are their homes like?

_____

_____

What are some of the ways they earn a living?

_____

_____

Draw a picture to show a typical family and their home.

African Music

Music has always been an important part of African life. Traditionally music was a part of all ceremonial and social events. When people of the same ethnic or cultural group came together, music and dance were a large part of the event. Music was even a part of group work experiences.

When Africans moved to other continents, they took their music tradition with them. In the Americas, black African slaves sang traditional African music. Over time this music became a part of American music as the basis of gospel music, jazz, and the blues.

Music and dance are still a strong part of ceremonial life in African cultures.

How do you think each of these instruments is played?

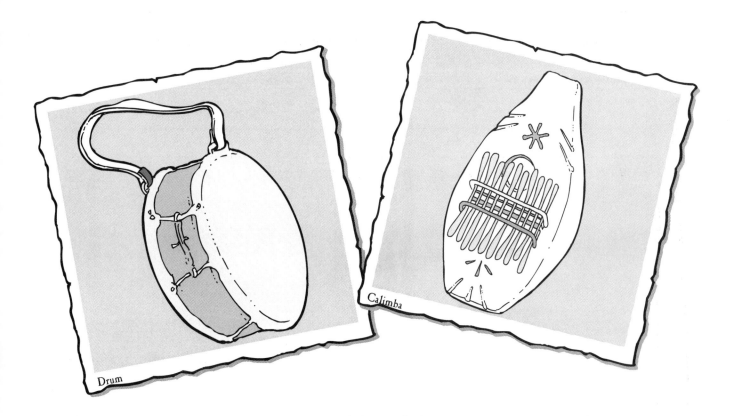

Drum

Calimba

African Art Forms

Baskets, pottery, beadwork, metal pieces, and fabric are examples of Africa's beautiful artwork. Traditionally these creations were functional items for daily use. Many of these same crafts are still practiced. Today some of the items produced are worn or used as household goods and decorations. Many are sold as art objects.

Exotic carved masks and figures were originally created for use in rituals. Today you will find them in galleries and museums featuring fine African art.

Tanzanian beadwork

Bonus

Think of something you use that could be considered a work of art. Describe it or draw it here.

Celebrate Learning

Choose one or all of the following activities to celebrate the culmination of your unit on Africa. Use the activities to help assess student learning.

Have a Portfolio Party

Invite parents and other interested people to a "portfolio party" where students will share their completed portfolios, as well as other projects about Africa.

Write a Book

A student can make a book about Africa. It might be one of the following:
* an alphabet book of African people, places, or plants and animals
* a dictionary of words pertaining to Africa
* a pop-up book of the unique animals of Africa

Conduct an Interview

A student can interview someone from Africa or someone who has visited there. The interview could be in person, written about, or videotaped to share with the class.

Create a Skit

One or more students can write and present a skit about an interesting event or period in African history.

Paint a Mural

One or more students can paint a mural showing one region of Africa. A chart of facts about the region should accompany the mural.

Share an Artifact Collection

Students can bring in one or more artifacts representative of Africa such as an art object. A written description of each artifact should be included in the display.

Name _____

Africa

Relative location _____

Number of countries _____

Continent land area_____

Largest country by area

_____

Smallest country by area

_____

Continent population _____

Largest country by population

_____

Smallest country by population

_____

Highest point _____

Lowest point _____

Longest river _____

Largest island _____

Interesting facts about the continent's regions:

* _____
* _____
* _____
* _____
* _____

Interesting facts about the people:

* _____
* _____
* _____
* _____
* _____

Interesting facts about the plant and animal life:

* _____
* _____
* _____
* _____

Name

What's Inside This Portfolio?

Date	What It Is	Why I Put It In

Name

My Bibliography

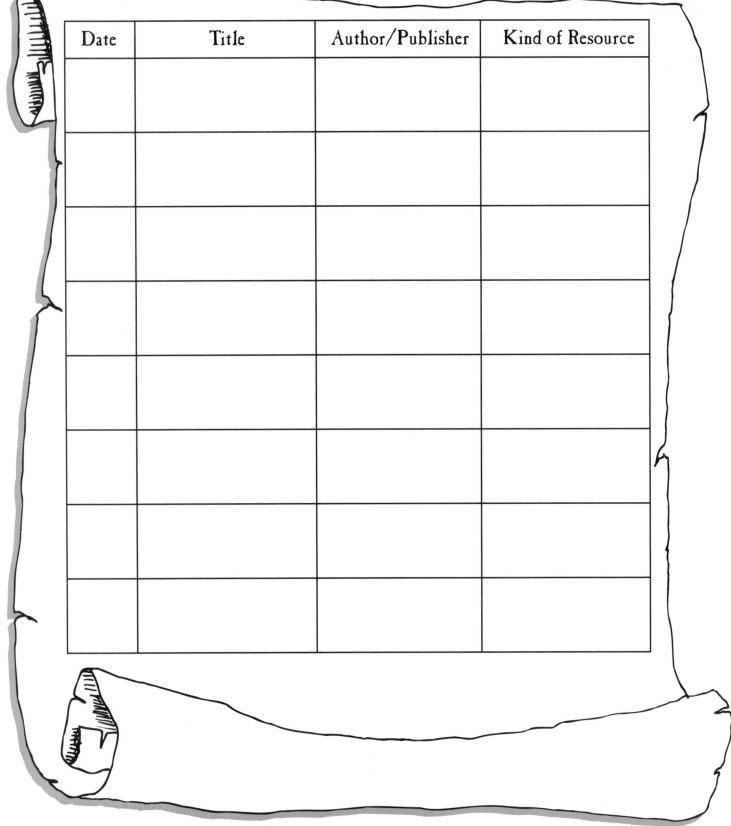

Date	Title	Author/Publisher	Kind of Resource

Search _____

What is the longest river in Africa?

How long is it?

1

Search _____

What is the largest lake in Africa?

In what country or countries is it located?

2

Search _____

Which African country has three capital cities?

Name the cities and their functions.

3

Search _____

What is the highest mountain in Africa?

How tall is it?

4

Search _____

What countries in Africa touch the Mediterranean Sea?

5

Search _____

What is the name of the cape at the southern tip of Africa?

6

Search _____

What is the biggest difference between a dromedary camel and a bactrian camel?

7

Search _____

Name this animal and tell where it is found.

8

Search _____

Name the large island country in the Indian Ocean off the coast of Africa.

9

Search

Name this monument. In which country is it found?

10

Search

Which African countries does the equator pass through?

11

Search

What is the lowest point in Africa?

What is its elevation?

12

Search

In what ocean will you find the island of Madagascar?

13

Search

Which of these three countries has the smallest land area: Eritrea, South Africa, or Togo?

14

Search

What animal is called the "ship of the desert"?

How is it used?

15

Search

What desert covers a large part of Botswana?

16

Search

What river forms one of the borders between Congo and Democratic Republic of the Congo?

17

Search

Where does the lowest amount of rainfall in Africa occur?

18

Africa • EMC 769

What are the ancient tombs of Egyptian kings called?

19

Is Africa larger or smaller in land area than Asia?

20

Which of these lines of latitude run through Africa?

   equator
   Tropic of Cancer
   Tropic of Capricorn

21

Which oceans and seas border Africa?

22

The largest desert in the world is in Africa. What is the desert's name?

23

How many countries (including island countries) are there in Africa?

24

On what river will you find the Victorian Falls?

25

Why is Olduvai Gorge important to archaeologists?

26

What is the name for a place with water and plants growing in a desert?

27

Name

Africa

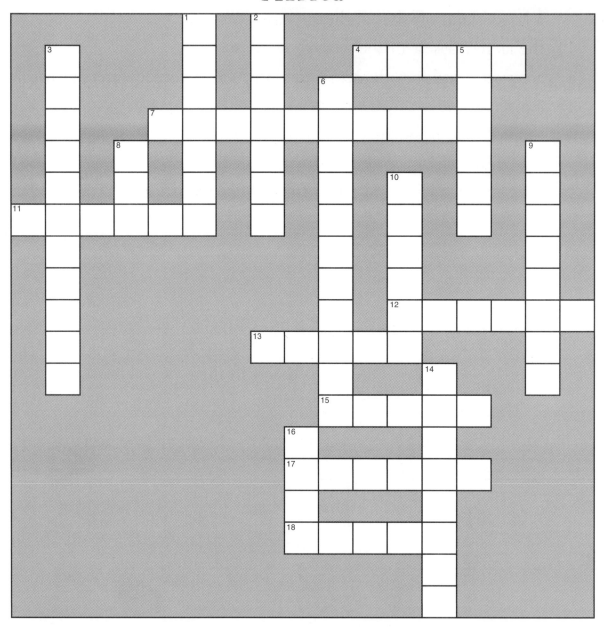

Word Box

Africa	Kilimanjaro	Sahara
Atlantic	Madagascar	savanna
desert	Nile	Sea
Egypt	nomads	south
equator	oasis	Sudan
Indian	rainforests	Victoria

Africa • EMC 769